The Male Mysteries Rites & Rituals For The Journey To Manhood

Nikki Dorakis

Foreword by M M C Fraser

ISBN: 1500996858
ISBN-13: 978-1500996857

Dedicated to the Memory of

Nikki Dorakis (1954-2013)

CONTENTS

ACKNOWLEDGMENTS

I would like to thank my husband Richard, for talking me repeatedly through the image editing process, and to the Pagan Elders in Glastonbury and beyond for their valuable comments regarding some of the issues raised by the text. And to Adrian Sparkes, David Kreps, Carla Haygarth, and all of those who gave me the help and encouragement I needed to finish editing and finally publish this work.

Special thanks to Gracie & Roberto Salazar, who together with others, arranged for the original material to be scanned and sent to me from Spain. Without their kindness, the publication of this book would never have been possible.

Invokation of the God (Page 77) written by Doreen Valiente in her book "Witchcraft for Tomorrow" and reproduced here with the kind permission of the publishers, Robert Hale Ltd.

FOREWORD

By M M C Fraser

This book was originally produced in the form of a hand written and illuminated Grimoire. Where possible I have kept closely to the original format of the text and I have included a number of the original illustrations. None of the original wording has been changed, however, I used editorial changes to clarify where appropriate or to indicate where a word was not legible. Such changes are marked thus [ ] and where editorial notes are given for each chapter at the end the book they are marked numerically thus [ ]¹ In addition, because the work was produced by hand some items were added out of sequence. In order to lend clarity and maintain the logical flow of the text, I have adjusted this accordingly.

On editing the book I took the opportunity to discuss a number of the points raised within it with Pagan Elders, as a result of which important questions were raised concerning the philosophical viewpoint of the author expressed in Why We Need The Rite of Passage (Chapter 1) with regard to the feminist movement, and also the lack of reference to the transgendered community, in particular female to male transgendered people, and their access to the rituals contained within the text. It seems pertinent to deal with these issues here.

The 'Feminism Question'

In my many discussions on feminist issues with Nikki during his life, it was clear that he was a believer in equality between the sexes but had become increasingly frustrated with what he saw as the portrayal of traditional 'male' qualities as undesirable, in particular that male sexuality was seen as aggressive and domineering. Although he was aware of the root causes of these assertions, his view was that something had to be done to increase the value of manhood both in the eyes of society as a whole and for men in particular; whilst at the same time ensuring that young men were encouraged to move away from the premise that the ideal man would develop the negative use of males skills and see them as a positive attribute. For example, the use of physical strength to dominate the weak rather than to protect them. Unless this was achieved he felt that society would see the continuing decline of the male into either the "eunuch" or the "thug" each being equally undesirable; when we should be striving towards the development of a well-rounded, multifaceted individual who could show aggression if necessary, but who could also show love and compassion without worrying about appearing weak. To this end he moved towards the idea of the formation of Brotherhoods, or the Company of Men.

Although the exclusion of women in the creation of an exclusively male domain would be the inevitable result, it is not the primary intention. The intention is clearly stated: "The Rite of Passage and the Company of Men exists precisely to create the circumstances and environments which foster and nurture the qualities of positive Manhood." The Company of Men would enable a structured progression from boy- to man-hood assisted by those who had personal experience of the physical, psychological, spiritual, and sexual processes involved. I think we can all agree the point that a woman can never experience what it means to be a man, and vice versa. His issue was not with feminism per se but with the "ideals of feminism ignorantly applied". (See Chapter 1) That is, the attempt to raise one gender above the other which, in his view, had no place within the Company of Men and should not have a place within society as a whole.

It is clear when reading the book that in today's society, female support rather than permission, for the Company of Men would inevitably be required. For instance, encouraging the formation of safe, positive male relationships can be problematic for single mothers, much as they would like to be able to do so. The involvement of any male under the age of 16 with the activities mentioned within the book would obviously require the mother to be supportive and to have personal knowledge and relationships within a community which would allow her to safely release the child/young adult into the care of others. This would be the case regardless of gender. Large male group camping trips for example are more acceptable if a father or other male relative is present, but this is not always available and is an issue which would need to be addressed should any boy under 16 seek rite of passage. Mentorship in the absence of a father is an option - again this individual would need to be known to, and trusted by, the mother. My personal view is that in the light of the way our society is currently structured, any Rite of Passage should not be undertaken until age 16.

So should women be concerned about the prospect of a Company of Men? In my opinion, as a woman, I would say no and I would welcome it as a positive thing. That of course would largely depend on the views, activities and ethics of each individual Company. As with anything, such groups can be a force for good or ill. We currently enjoy a number of female only activities within society - like the Red Tent Groups that are becoming increasingly popular - which deal with issues of the female mysteries in a safe space with others who understand where we are coming from. Would we really seek to deny this for our men?

LGBT Issues Raised by the Book

Nikki was very clear that same-sex partnerships should be seen by society (and by the Company of Men) as what they are: as honourable, and as valid as male-female partnerships. Whom one chooses as a bed mate is a matter of no concern to anyone apart from those involved in the relationship. As is clearly demonstrated by the text, it is essential that personal relationships, sexual or otherwise, are based on mutual respect and equality.

So where does this leave Transgendered People? The text specifically states that *women* could not become part of the Company of Men. So where does that leave a female to male transgendered person seeking a spiritual rite of passage? Nothing within the book specifically deals with this issue, I obviously cannot seek Nikki's view on this, and I am certainly no expert in the subject, so I can only extemporise from our discussions and from my own personal experience and perspective. I believe that a male individual born into a female body who is transitioning to their true gender would benefit greatly from a Rite of Passage as detailed within the book. Rituals are extremely powerful on a personal psychological level and can be useful in marking the path of their transition. It would be possible to adapt the ritual slightly in order to meet their individual needs, depending on the point of their journey they are seeking to mark. Being accepted by a community in their true identity will also be a powerful affirmation, both for the individual concerned and for members of the community as a whole. As far as full admittance to the Company is concerned, speaking as a female, I personally would not see an issue and I have never experienced a problem with admitting a male to female transgendered person into an all-female group. I would hope that this would be repeated in this case, although ultimately it would be for each individual Company of Men to decide. If after reading this book anyone is inspired to write a ritual for transgendered people or would like to collaborate on a project of this nature, I would love to hear from you and can be contacted via the website.

M M C Fraser

Glastonbury, September 2014

Nikki Dorakis

PART ONE: RITES OF PASSAGE

1 WHY WE NEED THE RITE OF PASSAGE

Over the centuries we have allowed the formal Rites of Passage to vanish. This is much to our detriment both as a gender and a species. Bastardised remnants of the Rites linger on in the "hazing" practices engaged in by fraternity groups and in the high-jinx behaviour observable in all-male enclaves when a new or younger male seeks to join the group. The reasons that these remnants remain are, no doubt, complex; but simply put, men need to bond in groups and be formally recognised by [their][1] fellows.

During the Rites the Boy is seeking to move forward and embrace his approaching manhood, the ways of his fellows, the spirit of man, and his God. It is only once the boy is formally accepted by the Company of Men that his masculine identity is consolidated.

It is essential that there remain preserves that are exclusively masculine and which are structured by men expressly to nurture the spirit of men.

Boys, if they are to become stable and whole men, must learn to fulfil their natures and fully realise them before embarking on the quest for a mate – whichever gender they choose to court. They must know themselves as complete in their own right before giving themselves into any relationship requiring even partial surrender of their autonomy.

The Rite of Passage and the Company of Men exists precisely to create the circumstances and environments which foster and nurture the qualities of positive Manhood.

Already our educational system is failing our young males by emphasising aspects at which females excel to the exclusion of things at which males exceed. The conduct of our educators and the changes in the structure of our society undermines the essence of the male competitive spirit and its drive to develop leadership qualities. These characteristics have been systematically undervalued and reviled, no less so than by the evolution of the odious little eunuch – the New Age Male – who daren't even get an erection without the permission of a woman for fear of being thought aggressive. This is further compounded by the development of misanthropic attitudes born of the principle of feminism ignorantly applied.[2]

The loss of the proper masculine identity and ethics is what impels our youths to vent their frustrations in the violent and destructive behaviours we see almost daily on the television and in the newspapers.

A Man is defined not by what he owns or possesses. He is defined not by what he claims or promises – these things are merely Glamour. A Man is defined by what he does

2 THE PLANETARY INFLUENCES

The growth of the male from childhood to manhood is a complex process. The male child needs guidance through this process so that he understands the process of change and the responsibilities inherent with the advent of the abilities and power of manhood.

The changes occur both physiologically and psychically, materially and spiritually. This development is steady and inexorable, and the male should be guided throughout so that he is able to adjust to his changes properly and well. He must be helped to understand the significance of and responsibilities inherent in his superior strength; he must be made aware of his Duties and how these are linked to his Rights.

The developmental changes that signal the growth from Child to Man occur, in the first instance at the age of seven. This is when the spiritual and magical energies begin to move in his life.

NEPTUNE – YEAR SEVEN

Spiritual awakening begins in the male child's seventh year. It is at this time that he becomes more acutely aware of the transience of life. He begins to become aware of Death as a reality and an irreversible and "permanent" state. He will also become more aware of his own mortality at this point.

The Male Child begins to explore the world of religion and spirituality. He may start to show an interest in Magick. He will begin to develop theories and ideas about how the world "works" and start to develop a desire for understanding and philosophy.

At age seven the male undergoes his first major change at the cellular level. The body is said to regenerate in seven-year cycles, hence the most significant changes occur at seven, fourteen, and twenty-one. The significance given to the latter two ages of fourteen and twenty-one is very clear in many cultures, witness the traditions of Bar Mitzvah at the Talmudic "coming of age" [age 13][1] and the "key of the door" practice in western traditions at age twenty-one.

SATURN – YEAR EIGHT

In the Saturnium phase of the child's development, the upheavals of Neptune are beginning to resolve. Saturn's crystalising influence is affecting him on 2 levels:

On the physical level the body is settling into its new structure, adjusting to its growth spurt and to the alterations in hormone levels. Hand-eye coordination is being fine-tuned – periods of clumsiness may be observed due to growth changes altering the length and size of extremities. This is most noticeable at age fourteen.

On a spiritual level insights into life may be forming into spiritual or religious beliefs. The male child becomes more aware of the fragility of life, and may become preoccupied with thoughts of death and loss. He may be subject to periods of melancholy and worry about losing his parents or friends to death.

MARS – YEAR NINE

The Martian energy is that of Fire. The male child's inner warriors begin to awaken and rebellion against authority starts.

Disobedience is a wholly natural part of development, but it is an energy that must be controlled and very carefully managed. Self-assertion is a powerful master, but in the early stage of its development it is one that is easily slain. This is not the aim of discipline. The purpose of discipline is to temper and mould the inner warrior into positive, creative, and powerful qualities.

Males recognize gender differences much more quickly than females, and males naturally gravitate towards each other to form groups or gangs. This bonding is a powerful force, which if left unchecked or unguided will become Wildfire – the energy that fuels the delinquent roughians, who roam the streets engaging in the destructive, anti-social behaviours that form the stuff of news reports.

SOL – YEAR TEN

This is the time at which the solar energy returns to rekindle the fires of development in the male child. It awakes the first insights into the self-determination inherent in manhood.

It is at this time that the male child begins to break from the influence and authority of women, and starts to look to other males for direction, a sense of belonging, recognition, and approval.

Traditionally it was at this age that the male children left the Company of Woman and joined the ranks of Pages and Squires in the Company of Men. In this Company the boys learn how to become men.

In this year the male child develops morality and ethics. He has learned the difference between right and wrong and understands it. He can now make informed decisions regarding conduct.

Children at this age have the ability and capacity to be deliberately cruel and wicked and for the most part they are thoughtlessly self-seeking. The impulsive Martian Fire of Age 9 is blending into the Solar Fire which will become self-sustaining and which will ultimately forge the spirit of the boy into the character of the man.

Thus Fire must be brought under control and the development guided by adult males.

URANUS - YEAR FOURTEEN

At Year 14 the boy, now Squire, will have reached his second point of development. This coincides with the onset of puberty. The solar fire activates the Uranian energy causing the Squire to develop the desire to grow beyond his current state.

The final break from the physical constraints of boyhood [occurs][1] as his body begins to develop adult characteristics.

The influence of Uranus is that of chaos. It is the planet of the innovator, the eccentric. Its energy breaks old established patterns, overturns traditions, and demolishes obstacles to progress. It is not only a disruptive energy but also facilitative. Once the energy activates the old order is gone forever and the new order is founded.

At this second point of Initiation, the Squire becomes Apprentice and begins his learning of the ways of Men and of the significance of the changes taking place in his body. He will be educated regarding the responsible and safe enjoyment of these new attributes against and upon a foundation of ethical conduct and respect.

YEAR SIXTEEN

By year 16 the youth should be well versed in the attributes of his manhood, and, in demonstrating his understanding of his responsibilities, he shall be deemed ready and worthy to select a partner. The youth may pledge his troth, but he should be sure that he has the skills and income sufficient to support a wife and children if that is his chosen path – hence he should be advised not to act in haste – lest he repent at leisure.

Should he choose to partner himself with another male this shall be seen as an honourable liaison. He should be guided in this choice by the Company of Men, and the precepts by which we live. He should be guided by his heart as much as by his logic in ensuring that his chosen has skills and qualities that complement his own.

All partnerships are entered into in a spirit of mutual respect and the two shall conjoin as equals. Members of the Company may now pay court to a youth who has passed through the Third Gate.

3 THE MOVEMENT TO MANHOOD

The movement to manhood must be sought by the boy of his own volition. It cannot be sought on his behalf by another and neither can he be coerced into it.

He can be made aware of the advantages of moving into manhood. This is a gradual process, controlled and guided by the Company of Men, the boy's father or mentor, and the cleric. The boy will learn of and gradually take on the rights and responsibilities of manhood in a properly controlled, disciplined, and protected manner.

It is paramount to male development that a boy is formally recognised and taken into the fellowship of his adult counterparts. It is equally important that he should know from within and without that he has left his childhood, or boyhood, behind and that he now has a properly recognised place within both the adult male company and within the wider community circle. He must also come to the awareness at this time that his opinions and conduct have an effect on that community either for good or ill depending on what he does or says.

When a male child sues for Rite of Passage it is the responsibility of his father, or mentor, and the cleric (normally a Druid, Bard, or Arch-Druid) to ensure that the boy is properly prepared.

This preparation is carried out over the period of one, two or three lunar cycles. This commences from The Maiden crescent and culminates in the Crone crescent into the Dark moon.

THE PROTOCOL

A boy seeking Rite of Passage into the world of Men shall speak firstly to his father. In the absence of the father the child shall approach the man whom he respects above all others. This man shall be known as the boy's mentor or sponsor.

The father or mentor will then seek out the Arch-druid in his place and take the boy child to him at the appointed time. The boy will be seen alone.

The cleric will explain the seriousness of the request to the boy stressing that, once embarked upon, the path cannot be abandoned. The cleric must further satisfy himself that the boy is ready for the Rite and that there has been no coercion. He will ask the boy-child three questions three times:

Do you seek passage of your own will?
Do you understand that once you leave your childhood behind you cannot return to it?
Are you afraid?

The cleric must be satisfied that the boy has answered truthfully and that the child is sufficiently mature both emotionally and physically so that he will endure and manage such tasks as are set him as evidence of his fitness to pass into the Company of Men.

The boy-child should be able to demonstrate a reasonable degree of understanding of what he is asking for. He must be able to persuade the Cleric that he is seeking to grow in knowledge and ability and that he has a basic grasp of the responsibilities of manhood. He should also demonstrate a sensible degree of apprehension at the forthcoming change in his life.

The absence of this apprehension should be viewed as either hubris or lack of insight. Taking on one's manhood is a serious matter. An overly nervous candidate must receive the appropriate guidance and be told to return at a later date.

When the cleric is satisfied that the boy child is prepared he will give him a scroll or tract detailing the preparations that he must make and how he should conduct himself through the Rite. The boy child will commit the tract to memory. On the night of the rite this tract shall be burned together with the trappings of childhood.

No details of the Rite may be written, or disclosed to the Candidate.

PREPARATION OF THE CANDIDATE

The candidate will visit the Cleric twice each week on the day of the Sun and on the day of Mercury. During these visits the candidate will learn about The God and how he should conduct himself during his Becoming.

The Candidate will meet with his Mentor on the day of Jupiter or Mars to discuss the nature of Manhood – its Rights and Responsibilities.

The Boy should be set various tasks or duties suitable to his quest – such tasks might be the collection or preparation of firewood or collecting meat from the butchers. Whatever the tasks set they should be relevant to the role of Men as Hunter/Provider or Gatherer.

The boy should also be taught basic forest or trail skills, such as how to make fire, how to snare, and how to make a shelter.

RITUAL CLOTHING

Pre Rite

A simple thigh length tunic of linen, cotton, or wool in white. This garment is fastened at the shoulder by a ribbon or tape tie, and at the waist by a white sash or cord.

He will wear a white breech cloth and girdle underneath – plain white shorts otherwise.

He shall wear leather sandals.

Rite and Post-Rite

During the Rite the Candidate will shed the ritual white tunic and will receive his First Rite Clothing signifying his acceptance into the Company of Men as a Squire.

The First Rite Squire's garb is as follows:

> A white shirt of linen or cotton, having long sleeves
> Dark brown or black trousers
> A dark green tabard of wool
> A leather belt
> Strong boots or shoes

He will be presented with an amulet or pin of copper bearing the crest or sigil of the Company, and at this time he will take on the Circle Name – the name by which he will be known in the Company when it gathers. At the conclusion of the Rite, the Boy will be crowned with a circlet of woven ivy and oak.

4 INITIATION: THE PRECEPTS

A man's role is complex and must be explained carefully to the Initiate to ensure that he understands this complexity and will develop in the Way of Men under the guidance and support of his Mentor and, ultimately The Company. With this guidance and support he will come to understand, balance and control these complexities and the contradictions inherent in his Manhood.

The commentaries attached to the precepts intend to assist both Mentor and Cleric in their respective roles as aids in organising their thoughts and tutelage during the time of preparation. They are not definites and should not become dogma

SACRIFICE

Nothing can be accomplished without Sacrifice

Life itself is a process replete with conflicts. The process of Creation itself is a state both [of][1] conflict and sacrifice. The process requires by its very nature that certain components are destroyed or sacrificed so that other things may come into being. Even the process of Birth requires the destruction or sacrifice of both the sperm and ovum in order to forge new life. Some mystics – the ones that look at words like 'destruction' and view them as 'dark' – prefer to say that these substances have changed. They have not changed, however, because their original form and nature are lost at conception and cannot be recovered by any means.

"Change" implies that something of the original nature or character of a thing remains. This may apply to the processes of chemistry where components of compounds can be reclaimed as the original elements by the application of a chemical or other catalyst.

This basis process is one of creation and destruction – the original elements are recovered, but the compound (and sometimes the catalyst) is lost. The compound is in effect, destroyed – it has been sacrificed to obtain its components.

This allegory applies to the transition of the male from Child to Boy, Boy to Youth, of Youth to Man (Adult), and from Man to [Adult and][2] Sage.

When the child seeks his Rite Of Passage (as well as his Right of Passage), he is seeking to shed the things of childhood and embrace the things of manhood. Once the candidate steps through the forest gate and enters the World of Men, the Child is gone forever.

The man comes from the boy as surely as flame comes [from][3] fire, and as the type of fire is determined by the fuel that is used, the kind of man a boy will become is determined by the guidance he receives from the men he identifies and associates with.

CHARACTER

A man's character is forged by his reactions to the forces that act upon his life. His reactions are influenced by the 5 elements that inform his being. Our male nature comprises the five elements of creation and each is present in varying measure.

Fire – The Warrior & Leader

Fire imbues us with passion, drive, and ambition. It is the prime mover – the dynamo that powers Creation and which informs the energy of Life itself.

Water – The Mystic, Poet, Bard & Healer

Water imbues us with compassion, sensitivity and creative thought. Intuition is also governed by elemental water. Water is the universal conduit carrying knowledge and [has][4] the ability to cleanse.

Air – The Philosopher, Diplomat, Judge & Advocate

Air imbues us with inspiration and understanding. It is the foundation of logic and creative thought.

Earth – The Craftsman, Artisan, Farmer, & Hunter

Earth imbues us with the ability to manipulate matter, to build and create our environment. It gives the impetus to practical thought and practical skill.

Spirit – The Magician, Priest, Druid & other Magickal Types

Spirit aligns us into harmony with Creation. It imbues our elemental qualities and ourselves with virtue.

Not all men are warriors, just as we are not all mystics, healers, mages or hunters. We are composite creatures; our raw talents generally reflect the dominant elements in our natures. It is rare to find a man whose character is purely and completely aligned to one Element. We are by nature composite, as stated.

The great warrior leaders in our history are generally aligned to fire, some possessing a degree of air or water which gives them immense drive and charisma. Such men accomplish great things – often terrible things – but great nonetheless. Their lives are usually short, their deaths being as spectacular as their lives; and if not spectacular, then dramatic.

The Greeks referred to this quality as man's Daimon – the spirit or influences which informed his life and manifested in his actions and his behaviour.

In developing his character a man seeks to balance his elements so that he may invoke and channel his qualities as appropriate to the situations in which he finds himself and which will benefit both himself and his fellows.

HUNTER, GATHERER & PROTECTOR

Man is by nature a hunter. He will seek out his food and shelter and in these times his quarry is not so much the boar or stag, but a livelihood that enables him to provide for himself, his family and his community. And herein hangs a problem: we needs must re-establish the individual's sense of responsibility to his community, as well as to himself and his family.

In his role as gatherer in our modern world a man will gather resources in the form of money, possessions, or goods. This again, will enable him to fulfil his role as a provider.

His role of protector comes from his instinctual drives and the most specific instinct of territorialism. This is a deep seated instinct and where it is particularly strong in an individual it manifests as a career move such as the police or politics.

BALANCE

Take nothing from the world without giving something back in return.

The symbol of Jupiter is applied to this, the third precept, because it is the joining of the crescent moon of intuition and the cross of matter. Thus it represents the practical application of knowledge, understanding and skill. This application may be recognized as Wisdom, itself a quality of the Jupiterian energy.

A man's skills are graces bestowed by the process of Creation and through Evolutionary change that results from this process. To avoid the pitfalls created by hubris, we must always remember that we are the conduits for these abilities and not their owners.

"We can but do that which is ours".

A man manifests balance by using skills and talents to benefit both himself and his community. By this action he is returning something to the World in recognition of what the World has given him. As a result of this 'giving back' [in this way][5] a man's level of skill and his ability to provide for his family will increase.

The same process of balancing can be seen in the old methods of farming and husbandry – what is not needed is ploughed back into the land as compost. There is no waste – any surplus can be given to those in need,

23

and thus Balance is honoured and maintained by providing succour and support where it is lacking.

Modern attitudes towards effort are sadly lacking in any idea of giving, and it seems that the modern ideal is to get as much from the world or one's fellows as possible whilst expending a minimum of effort or investment. To maintain the notion and quality of Balance and honour it – a man should remember that time is not money and his life is not worth its weight in gold.

If something is worth doing then it is worth doing to the best of a man's ability – this requires effort. The result is the production of an artefact or circumstance of note and worth, for it will only be valued according to the effort invested in its creation. This will be true both for the artisan and those who benefit from his labours. Effort expended is redressed by the just pride in achievement, recognition, and praise. The sweat of human endeavour is the succour of the gods – it gives their lives flavour and lets them know their Graces are appreciated.

It is inherent in a man's nature that he appreciates, values and respects those things he has striven for or invested something of himself in. This may explain the current trend of disregard for the welfare of the community and the get-what-you-can mentality prevalent amongst certain groups in Society.

Contribution to the lives and welfare of others is a choice and none may insist that a Man does it. A Man who shirks this ethical responsibility has no right to expect support from a community to which he contributes nothing.

BROTHERHOOD

All men are brothers. We are joined by the collective of our gender
and by the divine fire that informs our existence.

Our Brotherhood is a sacred unity. We must maintain it at all costs and we must never be divided or separated by any means.

Let those who set brother against brother beware. Those who manipulate brotherhood into malice and enmity are to be reviled, disgraced and expelled from the Company of Men, until such time as they have made good and repented their actions.

No greater tragedy can befall the Company of Men than that they should go to war against and kill their brothers.

STRIFE

The existence of Strife in the Brotherhood and Company of Men is a completely natural phenomenon.

Men will argue and we will debate; we will compete against each other in matters of skill, strength, prowess and love. This is our nature. It is our heritage and it is to be revelled in and enjoyed in the spirit of mutual respect.

In victory a Man is gracious and respectful of his opponents – mindful always that it is only through them that he has come to shine.

In defeat a Man is not rancorous in his disappointment but salutes and enjoys the victory of his Brother and seeks to see in the victor the level of skill to which he himself aspires.

Though strife is a natural occurrence in us, we must be cautions of it. The Five of Wands appears here above as a warning. It warns against allowing our passions to overcome our reason. The Venusian, Arian and Saturnian wands form the rune Haegl, the rune of disruption. The wand of Saturn is seen to be shattering the wind of Elemental fire, forming the inverted rune of Tir ($\downarrow$) the rune of the spiritual warrior. This inversion symbolizes the corruption of our spirit of natural respect by the egocentric desire for personal advancement regardless of the cost to others.

In its positive form Strife, though by its nature disrupts, is also a creative process which opens us to growth and development. This is a result of our natural proclivity to compete and debate – this is a growth process when conducted in an atmosphere of mutual respect: and through this process, and in this spirit, though we may differ and disagree, we shall never be divided.

OF WAR AND KILLING

There is no greater darkness that can engulf us and no greater tragedy that can befall us than that we rise brother against brother and wage war.

We are brothers joined by the Spirit and our common form is seen in our physiology and shared attitudes. Our duty is to respect and love one another, and to live in a spirit of mutual support and cooperation.

War is anathema to our Spirit of Brotherhood. It is the single greatest darkness that can engulf us and the greatest tragedy that can befall us. It is a circumstance that must be averted at all costs. Peace should be sought urgently and earnestly by those Peacemongers within the disagreeing factions.

When men have had to go to war they must be brought back into the bosom of their community welcomed, hailed and treated with kindness and caring – for though they may have survived the battles, their wounds will be severe in terms of the damage done to their psyches and the injury inflicted on their souls. They must be helped to find their humanity again.

THE IMPERATIVE TO SURVIVE

This imperative is sometimes considered to be the strongest drive in a man – stronger even than love or the imperative to procreate. The preservation of the Self is the most basic of our instincts. A man will kill to preserve his life and the lives of his family through whom he is preserved in posterity.

Although we recognise the power of this imperative and its nature, and killing of a brother must be brought to the Company for judgment. The man must also be judged according to the Law of the Land.

Those adjudged as murderers shall be driven from the Company and shunned by the community. Only by unanimous agreement of both the Company and the elect of the community can a murderer be readmitted into our fellowship.

MURDER, SELF-DEFENCE AND MANSLAUGHTER

We cannot create Life and have no Right to take it in Murder.

A man may become disassociated from his brothers by many means and for many reasons. In the disassociated state he may develop designs to kill his brother that he may have his wife or his possessions. It may more simply be that he wishes to deprive his Brother of the life he covets for himself.

In circumstances of conflict it may be that the aggressor himself is destroyed. This must be seen as the consequences of the Aggressors actions and no blame can be attached to the man for defending his life.

The defender's brothers should grieve with him that he was forced to such an abhorrence, in order to preserve his life against such treachery. Equally they should grieve with each other for the Brother who was lost to Darkness. The company shall light candles, lamps or fires for his spirit that it should heal and the lamps shall light his path and guide him on his way.

A man who murders a child is to be expelled and forgotten. His name shall never be mentioned and all evidence of his presence shall be expunged from the Company.

5 ETHICS

A Man is honourable and honest in all his dealings. He does not seek to advance himself at the expense of his Brother. Men do not take advantage of the weaknesses or others, but seek to protect those who may be exploited by the unscrupulous. There is no price a Man will not pay to protect the weak. This is the root and foundation of our Honour and Strength as Spiritual and profane Warriors, and Love is the foundation of our Ethics Wheel: the topmost point of the Ethics Pentagram.

Ethics

Bindrune ᚠ: Wunjo-Sowelu~Wholeness & Joy:- ~: Love.

Mannaz ᛗ: The Self which must be the embodiment of our truths.

Tir ᛏ: Spiritual Warrior~Guardian of Honour.

Jera ᛃ: Justice~the Karmic cycle.

Gebo X: Partnership~Brotherhood~Peace.

The Bindrune is the combination of Wunjo and Sowelo (Wyn & Sigel). This represents love through joy and wholeness – each feeding the other in perfect harmony and balance within the crescent moon representing the soul and the red disc representing the Divine Fire that is *Primium Mobile* – the Prime Mover. As Men, Love is our motive and motivation. It is our inspiration – our *raison d'etre*.

Mannaz (Man) – the rune symbolising the profane self of the body. Love is our Prime Mover – the Truth of all Truths – we are vehicles. Our physical and spiritual selves manifest our philosophical, spiritual and mundane truths. This process manifests as Right Action or, as we see it – as Honour.

Teiwaz (Tir) – The Spiritual Warrior. He is the part of us that inspires us to manifest truth and justice. It is our sense of honour that prompts us to challenge and rise up against those things which threaten our unity and the principles by which we live.

Jera (Jer) – the cycle of the year. Also the Rune of Harvest. By extrapolation it symbolises reaping what is sown. In the Ethics Wheel it is the symbol of justice, karma and balance.

It is the love of Truth and the practical pursuit of Honour that upholds Justice. A Man does not uphold justice by applying the Letter of the Law alone. He must apply the Spirit of the Law in accordance with the principles of honour and the pursuit of Truth. Law considers only evidence: Justice considers the circumstances and influences inherent in the situation.

Gebo (Gyfu) – the rune symbolising partnership, joining and cooperation. It is a representation of the Two of Swords – truce. Peace arises through truth, honour and justice. It is peace that completes the cycle of ethics and returns to love.

Though Love is our motivator, Truth is our founding principle, for Men do not lie. To say a thing is when it is not or to see evil and call it good mocks the divine and spits on our most revered precepts. But what is worse is that when he lies a Man murders a part of the World and makes Goodness meaningless. A word with no meaning is a dead thing, a blasphemy, and it will inevitably pass out of understanding. When this happens then the very thing the word stands for passes out of the world and, if there is no champion of honour and truth to challenge the lie, it will be lost forever.

A lie seeks to destroy Truth and this breaks the ethical cycle:

> Without Truth there is no Honour,
> Without Honour there is no Justice
> Without Justice there is no Peace
> Without Peace there is no Love.

The broken ethical cycle is not irreparable and the man who breaks his cycle must begin the reclamation of his ethical state by redevelopment of the virtue that was lost. Aristotle asserts that ethical virtues are like skills and crafts – they are acquired and developed through practice and habituation; it therefore follows that lost elements can be re-taught or re-acquired. This, however, can be a very long process.

MORALITY

Our ethical nature is, in part, an innate state of being – almost an instinct borne from man's need to survive. The behaviours needed to cement and maintain relationships or hunting agreements or even those pacts for mutual protection – would form the foundation of the concept of ethics.

Morality on the other hand results from deliberations based on reason and logic, as much as it comes from our desire to be well regarded by our companions-in-arms and our community.

Morality concerns itself with what is good or bad and right or wrong. Where our ethical nature prompts us and even drives us towards what is right and decent; when the decision is made to act or not to act this determines its moral nature.

Our "virtue" is recognised from the choices we make and manifest through our actions – or the means we use to reach an end. Our morality is recognised in the same way. Thus since to act virtuously is a matter of choice so it is [also][1] in our power to act in vice, and where we can choose morality we can also choose to be immoral.

Where it falls in our power to do a thing when it is right; similarly if it is in our power not to do a thing (or even the same thing) when it is wrong, doing right or wrong being the essence of being good or bad is, in our power – it is thus in our power to be decent or reprehensible.

A Man's morality can only be reliably judged against the precepts and values held by our Company and Community as exemplifying those positive and creative qualities that manifest goodness.

Morality is not defined by personal choices that do not affect the well-being of the Company or community. Therefore a man's choice of partner or bed-mate is not for judgement or criticism providing the partnership is founded on the accepted codes of conduct and the company's accepted precepts.

In this regard, a man does not use his superior strength or guile to the detriment of his fellows. He does not take advantage of the innocence of youth. In seeking a bed-mate he is open and truthful of his intentions and respectful of the company he is courting.

SPIRITUALITY

Do as though wilt and it harm none, not even thyself[2]

When seeking to express his spirituality a man must discover the nature of his relationship with the Divine. Having reached this understanding, the man expresses this in accordance with his inner truth.

The way in which a man expresses this relationship is in any way he chooses that does not conflict with the above Rede[3] or break the Ethical Cycle, for the Divine Spark does not seek to cause chaos or harm.

In our quest for spirit and spirituality there are many pitfalls. We must remember at all times that not all spiritual men are benevolent – some are diametrically opposed to both the spiritual progress of the man and the resulting fellowship we may develop with Creation. The reasons for this are manifold and need not be examined here.

Our expression of spirituality is influenced both by our moral and ethical natures. In turn these qualities are influenced by the quality and [….][4] of our spiritual natures. It is therefore important to have a sound moral and ethical foundation before embarking on the quest for Spirit.

The weakest link in our quest for Spirit is the Profane Self or Ego. Problems will inevitably arise for the Seeker as soon as the ego intervenes believing it can do better than the natural processes, or if pride corrupts a virtue of the ethical cycle.

One of our greatest stumbling blocks is the notion that having the knowledge of good and evil makes us reliable judges of which is which. Thus we can be led to revere those things or people who meet our highly specialised (and equally unreliable) criteria for those who are good and worthy and those who are not.

DEATH

All things in the world must die. All things must pass away out of existence, each in accordance with its type. A man should keep death daily before his eyes – not so that he should be morbid or miserable, but that he should live his life to its fullest, missing no opportunity to bring joy and love to those around him. And he should remain mindful that in this present form he will pass this way only once.

From the dust of ages came our bodies; from the dust of ages came all forms. To the dust of ages shall that form return. And thus it is with the male that:

> The Child dies to give rise to the Boy
> The Boy dies to give rise to the Youth.
> The Youth dies to give rise to the Man.
> The Man dies to become the Elder and Sage.
> And in turn these die to become the Ancestors.

The eighth precept is the precept of crystallisation. It is the stage of finality whereby a thing fulfils is nature and returns to the Divine in its pure form.

In approaching Death a man must be of clear mind. He has an inalienable right to leave his life with dignity and honour. He has the right to determine his manner and time of death should nature deal him a circumstance he finds unacceptable.

If a man is unable to act within his own power to end the life he finds unacceptable he may prevail upon a member of the Company to assist him. Whether the comrade agrees to this or not is between him and his conscience. None in the Company may have any criticism to offer nor any right of comment unless it is sought.

Where the Company will offer support and understanding for the chosen action, the Man must be aware that the Law of the Land my not be sympathetic if he is called to account by its agents.

REBIRTH

All things will decay into the dust of ages from whence they come and from the dust of ages shall they return – remade in new form. From the dust of ages do we rise. We are united by form, by matter, and by spirit. We are as old as the Universe and, if we choose, as wise and knowing.

In Death and decay not a single atom is wasted; in rebirth not one jot of us is ever lost.

Here end the commentaries.

PART TWO: RITUAL

AS we approach Manhood so the God draws closer to us, and awakens in us All of our drive and passion; our nobility, our honour and with it our capacity for Darkness

6 RITUAL

The energy of the developing male is powerful and unpredictable. It causes the young and inexperienced male to behave impulsively.

Male energy can only be successfully controlled by other males. It interacts with and channels with the female or Goddess energy on its own predetermined terms, and cannot be controlled or directed by woman. Interactions between the male and female energy occurs by mutual consent and cooperation – neither is subject to the will of the other.

The Rites and Rituals inscribed herein are exclusive to Men, their Apprentices and Squires. Where women may enter the Company of Warriors, they may not enter or otherwise encroach upon the Company of Men.

Male Rituals do call on the offices of females on special occasions. In some practices males who were of proper age would be taken to appointed placed where he would give up his virginity to a maiden from a cognate homestead. His other sexual education would have already been completed in the Company of Men as appropriate to his needs and as requested by him.

CRONE

It may seem strange to find the Crone in an exclusively Male grimoire, but it must be remembered that man is born of woman. The Crone understands endings and new beginnings. She is the maiden who births us, the mother who nourishes us and the devourer who removes the old form to make room for the new.

In the Rites of Initiation the Crone takes up the child energy to allow the Boy to emerge when he is taken from the Earth at the appointed placed. Thus it is with all the Initiations that the Crone will be present to provide the trans-mutational energy.

THE GATES

The Gates that mark the way to the Appointed Place are markers. They are the thresholds delineating between where one life ands and the new life begins.

The Three of Wands shows the Seeking standing at a new horizon. The Gates themselves are constructed from three staves symbolising the new start – the treading of a new path..

When the initiate walks through the archway he is leaving his old life behind and embarking on the new one.

The Four of Wands is the card of Completion itself, the closing of one chapter of life and the opening of the next.

THE GATHERING PLACE

A place of gathering shall be chosen seven full days before the Crone Moon. It should be close to the Appointed Place but not in view of it.

There should be a central hearth and sufficient wood to last the night. The revellers should bring food and drink, and there should be a Bard or other musicians to bring music.

The Gathering can begin at any time during the day, but should not start later than sunset or as the moon rises showing the final crescent.

An archway should be constructed from three wooden staves to mark the entrance to the Appointed Place. This is the Forest Gate.

The Structure of the Gate

The Gate is constructed from three staves – two staves form the uprights, the third forms the crossbar. The uprights must not be driven into the ground but held up by six guide ropes of hemp or other natural fibre. These guides are secured by means of wooden pegs.

For the first Rite it can be constructed from Yew, Apple, Hazel, or Birch.

THE FOREST GATE

The Forest Gate is the doorway between worlds, this is why the stanchions must not pierce the earth.

The First Gate for the passage of the Boy is decorated with Ivy and Yew springs. (The Yew can only be cut with permission of the Driad, and a suitable offering should be left at the foot of the tree).

The six guides are dyed as follows:

1 Black
1 White

The remaining four are dyed for the Elements:

1 Red (Fire)
1 Green (Earth)
1 Yellow (Air)
1 Blue (Water)

The white rope is fastened to the left stanchion, the black to the right. The elemental guides are fastened Fire with Air [on the left][1], and Earth with Water [on the right][2]. The guides are used on all three gates.

Two torches are kindled either side of the gate, and a narrow trench filled with water shall mark the threshold. This trench should he hewn with either a bronze, bone, or wooden tool. No iron should be used to pierce the ground at the Gathering Place.

THE SECOND GATE

For the Rite of Passage for ages fourteen and sixteen the Gate is constructed of Oak. It is decorated solely with sprigs of oak. From the centre of the crossbar there should be hung a representation of the Stag God. At age sixteen the Gate is decorated as above with the addition of a bouquet of Yew and Mistletoe.

THE THIRD GATE

This is constructed of Yew staves for the Passage of Man to Elder. The guide ropes for the Gate are purple. The Gate is decked with sprigs of Yew and Holy woven into garlands using Ivy.

The threshold trench for this gate is filled with a mixture of water and red wine. Each Elder will add a drop of his blood to the trench as will the initiate when he approaches the gate.

7 INITIATION: THE RITE

The Rite of Passage should occur in concert with the phases of the moon.

Just as the candidate prepares himself during the waning moon, so his Passage will take place as the last sliver of the Moon is visible – that is about one hour before the Moon passes into full darkness or Crone phase. This is the time when the Crone/Devourer energy is at its zenith.

This last sliver of light represents the last glimmer of the Candidate's childhood – before it is extinguished by the Devourer.

Traditionally Rites of Passage would take place over many days, sometimes weeks. Boys would be sent on quests, set tasks and challenged to duels by more experienced older youths. In the modern world it is not always possible and neither is it practicable to set aside days at a time for the Rites to be conducted. It is with this in mind that, wherever possible, the Rites are set to take place over a weekend – commencing on the Friday evening and concluding on sunrise of Sunday morning. This timing, though more convenient, is governed by the moon being in the proper phase.

RIGHT ATTITUDE

It is in human nature to wish to do only those things which are convenient. Humankind as a species has become averse to effort. The effort applied in organising and conducting the Rites is paramount to both the significance and effectiveness of the Rites.

As with all magickal work, how one approaches the work will determine how successful it will be. Yet of more consequence, perhaps, is the attitude inherent in man; in that it is the nature of Men that they value only those things they have to struggle to attain. A boy will not value his Rite of Passage if those males conducting it do not make it a thing of virtue both for him and themselves. It is therefore essential that the Rites are approached respectfully and seriously, and that no corners are cut for the sake of expedience.

RIGHT EFFORT

Where the structure of the ritual, the order of the ceremony and the manner in which the Rite is conducted may be adjusted and designed to suit the participant, the elements of the Ritual may not. The Ritual's Elements are immutable – they cannot be negotiated and must be present in appropriate form and degree if the Initiation is to succeed.

THE CHALLENGES

The whole system of the Rite of Passage is a series of challenges. Without challenge there is no impetus to move, improve or develop.

The first challenge faced by the Initiate is his own growth process. A boy child brought up with the Precepts and Ethics of the Company is more likely to actively seek initiation into the Company than one who is not. It is the doom of the male, however to seek acceptance and recognition of his own gender one way or another. How creative or destructive this process will be depends on how well or poorly he is guided by parents and mentors as well as the kind of company he chooses in his peers. The process of initiation into manhood should therefore be one of guidance and education, challenging the Initiate to discover those qualities that are best in himself and in those around him and bring those qualities to the fore.

ELEMENTAL FEAR

A man does not surrender to his fears and neither does he allow his limitations to imprison him. Rather he will learn to face them and understand them – and by this means will overcome them.

Where fear is, mastery is not. Without fear man cannot know courage, for it does not take courage to act when one is unafraid. Courage comes from acting despite one's fears.

The Boy must have an appropriate level of fear in his heart when he comes to the Gathering Place, and no less so when he hears the sound of the winding horn that summons the Men to the Appointed Place.

He should be suitably afraid when he leaves his mother at the Gathering's hearth, and that fear should remain when he approaches the Forest Gate and is challenged by the Crone and his mentor/father.

This same fear should persist while he is walking to the appointed place alone and in the dark of the woodland – and continue through the Ritual until it is concluded.

THE APPOINTED PLACE

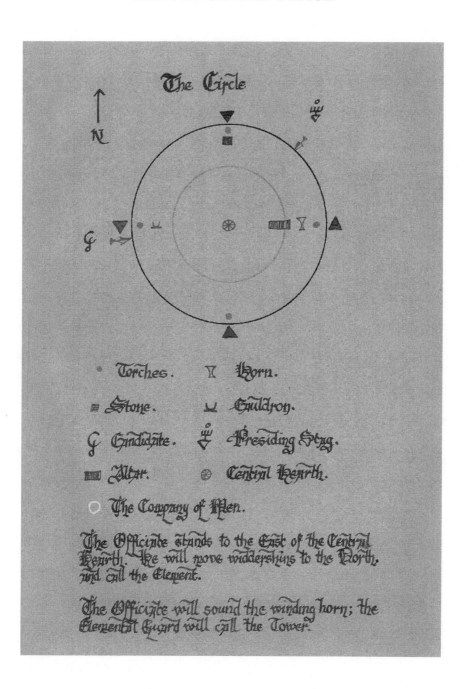

The Circle

- • Torches.
- ▦ Stone.
- G Gindidyte.
- ▥ Altar.
- ○ The Company of Men.

- Y Horn.
- ⊔ Guldron.
- ⚲ Presiding Stag.
- ⊛ Central Hearth.

The Officiate stands to the East of the Central Hearth. He will move widdershins to the North, and call the Element.

The Officiate will sound the winding horn; the Elemental Guard will call the Tower.

INVOKING THE NORTH

Peace be to the North!

Hail to the Guardians of the Watchtower of the North, ye powers of Earth, spirits of Form and Creation. We greet thee and invite thee to join us in our Rite. Come join us – lend us your strength and protection.

Hail to thee [.....][1] Lord of the Northern Watch, Guardian of Ice and Balance. We greet thee and ask you to attend our Rite to lend your grace, strength and protection. We ask that you witness our work, that it is virtuous and proper.

We bid thee hail and welcome!

INVOKING THE WEST

Peace be to the West!

Hail to the Guardians of the Watchtower of the West, ye powers of Water, spirits of Brotherhood and Intuition.. We greet thee and invite thee to join us in our Rite. Come join us – lend us your strength and protection.

Hail to thee [.....][2] Lord of the Western Watch, Guardian of the night. We greet thee and ask you to attend our Rite to lend your grace, strength and protection. We ask that you witness our work, that it is virtuous and proper.

We bid thee hail and welcome!

INVOKING THE SOUTH

Peace be to the South!

Hail to the Guardians of the Watchtower of the South, ye powers of Fire, spirits of Will, Determination and Passion. We greet thee and invite thee to join us in our Rite. Come join us – lend us your strength and protection.

Hail to thee [.....][3] Lord of the Southern Watch, Guardian of the Sacred Flame. We greet thee and ask you to attend our Rite to lend your grace, strength and protection. We ask that you witness our work, that it is virtuous and proper.

We bid thee hail and welcome!

INVOKING THE EAST

Peace be to the East!

Hail to the Guardians of the Watchtower of the East, ye powers of Air, spirits of Inspiration and Invention. We greet thee and invite thee to join us in our Rite. Come join us – lend us your strength and protection.

Hail to thee [.....][4] Lord of the Eastern Watch, Guardian of Wisdom and Illumination. We greet thee and ask you to attend our Rite to lend your grace, strength and protection. We ask that you witness our work, that it is virtuous and proper.

We bid thee hail and welcome!

THE CHALLENGE

"It is better that you should throw yourself upon this blade than to enter this Circle with a lie on your lips and falsehood in your heart.[5] And so I challenge thee in the name of this Company in the presence of those gathered here:-

How do you enter?

And the candidate shall respond:

I enter in perfect Love and perfect Trust."

SACRAMENTUM: 1

This oath is recited by the company of Men at every moot and formal gathering. The Sacramentum is repeated three times and can be spoken at either the start of the end of the proceedings.

If the discussions are particularly heated the Sacramentum, should be recited at the Closing as a means of reaffirming the bonds of the fellowship.

"We Swear in peace and Love to Stand,
heart to heart
and hand in hand.

Mark, O Spirit, and hear us now
Affirming this Our sacred vow."[6]

SACRAMENTUM: 2

THE PLEDGE

This oath is sworn by all candidates who join the Company of Men, whether he is concluding his Rites of Passage from Boy to Manhood or joining the Company as an adult male.

The blow that is struck at the swearing of the Oath should be of a strength and force that is appropriate to the Candidate but at the least sufficient to stagger him. When the Oath has been sworn each man in the Circle will offer the Candidate his blessing and conclude with the words:

"You knelt in this Company as a Boy, now rise as a man in the Company, as a man and one with us all."

Once the last blessing is made the Officiate will raise the Candidate to his feet and call out:

"All Hail the Man!"

And the Company shall respond:

"Hail the Man!"

THE OATH

To stand firm in the face of injustice –
To remain steadfast with your brothers and sisters through Adversity –
To speak the Truth though it cost you your life –
That there is no price you will not pay to protect the Weak –
Is this your solemn Oath?

The Candidate shall answer:

"Yes. This is my solemn Oath."

The Officiate will strike the Candidate across the face and thus having done will stand over him and say:

"And this shall help you remember it"

THE CHALICE RITE

The Rite is performed at all gatherings of The Company and at the commencement and conclusion of all moots. The drinking vessel may be a chalice, horn, stirrup cup or quaich. For the purposes of a moot the vessel is filled with mead. For Sabbats and celebrations of the God and Manhood, Ichor, Port or Stag's Blood is used.

The chalice is filled by the Officiate who will first pour a libation to the God and Goddess. He will then take a drink passing the vessel to the first to enter the Circle, with a kiss. The chalice is passed from each member in this manner Deosil around the Circle. A novice shall follow the chalice to refill it as required. By this Rite the fellowship of the Company is ratified and reinforced.

Each man of the Company shall possess a suitable flask which he will always carry in Circle. This flask shall contain Ichor or Stag's Blood made as detailed below. And when the flask is filled the man shall add one drop of blood or [his][7] own tears.

<u>Ichor</u>

200mls	Mead
100mls	Strawberry Wine
25mls	Cherry Brandy

<u>Stag's Blood</u>

200mls	Port
150mls	Mead
50mls	Vodka or Brandy

For the Mystery of Brotherhood each man shall add to the quaich or chalice one measure from his flask.

The vessel shall then be passed as in the Rite of the Chalice, with a kiss, and each shall recite the Invokation of Brotherhood as written.

THE INVOKATION

On taking the quaich and reciting the Invokation of Brotherhood, each celebrant will name the ability he would have that he sees in his brothers.

> I drink from you all gathered here - my Brothers - and unto myself I take....... [here the Brother will consider the quality that he sees in another Brother that he would like to develop in himself, and state it at this point][8]
> Blessed Be

> [The vessel is then passed to the next Brother, with a kiss][9]

8 CLEANSING THE SPACE

For each Rite and ritual the Appointed Place must be appropriately prepared and cleansed that it shall be fit for its purpose and suitable in the eyes of the Great Ones and to the eyes of the Company who meet and work therein.

Let therefore four Squires of the Company go into the Appointed place with besoms. There shall they encircle the enclave thrice about with brooms held haft to bristle. And have thus danced widdershins thrice about shall they gather all four at Quadrans Septentrionalis. [1]

Three shall then move to the remaining quarters in the form of the Awen thus forming the rune of the spiritual warrior as shown below. As they approach their quarters the three shall recite with their fourth:

"We come to cleanse this space to the honour of the Great Father, to the honour of the Great Mother, and to the honour of the Children of Creation. So mote it be!"

CLEANSING THE SPACE

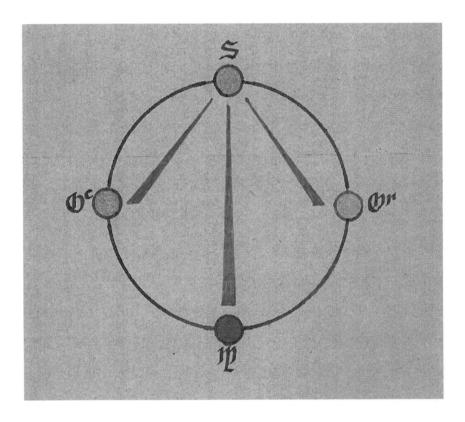

This shall be done quarter by quarter in the order in which the elements are to be invoked and this is determined by the nature of the Work to be undertaken.

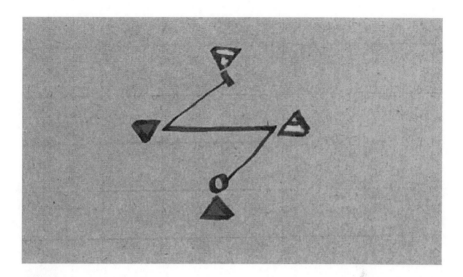

 Squire moves to the centre of the Circle and turns to face Meridiens[2] and says:

"I am Notus, Wind of the South, I come to cleanse this space by the Power of the Father and in Honour of the Mother"

The Squire begins to sweep from the centre of the circle to the boundary in scythe strokes moving all the debris and detritus towards the gap in the boundary stones. Whilst he sweeps the Squire will say:

"I am Notus, Wind of the South, breath of the Sacred Fire, before me no impurity shall stand but all shall be consumed, cleansed and transformed. In my wake shall remain only what is pure and true.

By the Great Father, this shall be so.

By the Great Mother, this shall be so.

By the Children of Creation, this shall be so."

As the oration is completed the Squire makes the final stroke expelling the detritus through the gap in the boundary stones. He says:

"So Mote It Be!"

And the other three shall respond: "So Mote it Be!"

 Squire will then move to the centre and turn to face Oriens.[3] He Says:

"I am Eurus, Wind of the East, I come to cleanse this space by the power of the Father and in Honour of the Mother".

He will sweep as per [the first Squire] Δ saying:

"I am Eurus, Wind of the East, Sword of Thought and Reason, the breath of truth and understanding. Before me no illusion can endure, ignorance and deceit, falsehood and treachery shall fall. In my path the clouds of illusion are dispersed. In my wake remains only what is pure and true.

By the Great Father, this shall be so.

By the Great Mother, this shall be so.

By the Children of Creation, this shall be so"

And on the last stroke the debris is expelled. [The squire says: "So mote it be!" And the other three shall respond as before.][5]

 Squire will then move to the centre and then turn to face Occidens.[4] He says:

"I am Zephyrus, Wind of the [West][6]. I come to cleanse this space by the Power of the Father and in Honour of the Mother.

He shall sweep as before saying:

I am Zephyrus, Wind of the [West][7], born of Fire and Air, I am the Breath of compassion, the Tears of Heaven. Before me no injustice or cruelty can prevail. My Waters temper the Sword of Reason and soothe the Fires of Passion. I am the Breath of Temperance. Before me all extremes are softened, stone hearts are renewed and obstacles are washed away. In my wake is calm and clarity and respect, only the purity of Compassion shall remain,

By the Great Father, this shall be so.

By the Great Mother, this shall be so.

By the Children of Creation, this shall be so."

And on the last stroke the debris is expelled. He says: "So mote it be!" and the others respond as before.

 Squire will move to the centre and turn to face Sephentrio.[8] He says:

"I am Aguilo, Wind of the North, Born of the Father and the Mother. I am the flesh and bone of the word, sacred ice without whom no thing may be. Before me none may stand. I will make mountains into plains and turns seas into deserts; I make gullies into rivers and turn tundra into forest. In my path, all is swept aside; in my wake is only Unity and Steadfastness as all is made anew."

And on the final stroke: "So mote it be!" And the others respond as before.

And with the Quadrants thus cleansed each Squire shall close the boundary with stone of the elemental colour and set the quarter candles or torches at the ready, to be lighted at the time of the calling. This being done they will exit the circle through the Seasonal Gate.

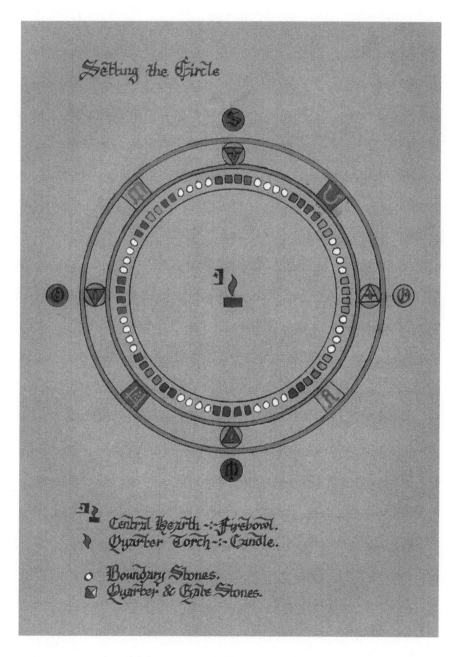

Setting the Circle

♪ Central Hearth -:- Firebowl.
♪ Quarter Torch -:- Candle.

o Boundary Stones.
▨ Quarter & Gate Stones.

From the Circle of Creation do we rise.
From the Circle of Creation all things do rise
Without the Circle there is nought

When your work in the forest is wrought your Circle shall be cast with this knowledge in your heart. All the Elements must work in accord:

Fire to Stir the Wind
Wind to stir the Water
Water to seed the Clouds
Earth to hold the Water
And bring forth growth that the Work may Become.

Cerneic Magicians work with the Land and in accordance with the Order of Creation. Thus do Cerns work always within the Structure of the World mindful always of the Ley wherein they work; never forgetting that the Elemental Quarters are governed by the Ley of the Land and not by the Compass.

The Circle is always set as a map. When in diagram form Septentrio is always at the top as with any cartographic work.

The geographical quarters are indicated outside of the bounding circle as shown above.

S = Septentrio - Arctus - North.
M = Meridies - South.
O = Oriens - East
O = Occidens - West.

9 COMMENTARY ON THE QUARTERS

The Seasonal Quarters are set between the Elemental Quarters so that if this outer boundary was set vertically it would chart the course of the sun through the Equinoxes and Solstices as it appears to pass from horizon to horizon.

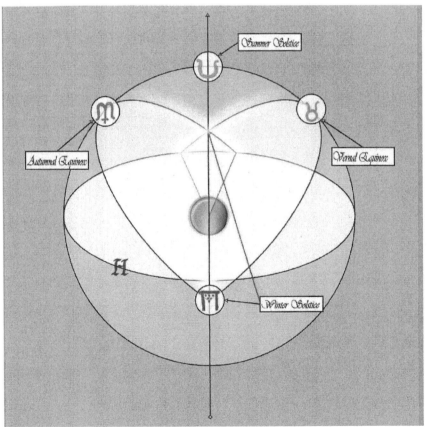

Figure 1

In the above representation [Figure 1] the Equinoxes are shown at halfway to the zenith that is Cuspis Solstitialis. The Winter Solstice is placed at the opposite side to the Summer showing the energy as being below the horizon {H}. The arrow indicates the "actual" nadir.

The map below [Figure 2] shows the Earth relative to the Sun at the Solstices and Equinoxes.

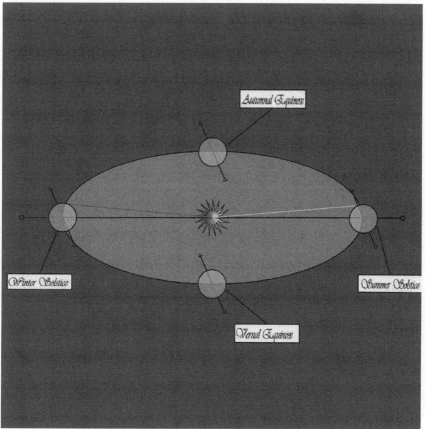

Figure 2

The Elements are set at the compass points to indicate when they exert their influences and demonstrate their qualities most fully.

- Fire is at its strongest at mid-summer. In the Northern Hemisphere the sun appears in the south as it travels east to west.
- Earth is placed in the north because it is at mid-winter matter it is at its most dense and inert state.
- Air is placed in the East to demonstrate its movement as it is warmed by the rising of the sun.
- Water is placed in the West because it is from here that the rains come carried by the winds.

The Circle is constructed with the seasonal gates located between the cardinal points of the roots of the elemental powers to demonstrate the flow of the energy of Creation.

From the Prime Mover the first stirrings are those of Spring as matter is warmed and activated by the transmutational power of fire.

As the creative force of fire increases Air begins its work giving intelligence and the directive force of reason to the Works of Nature and Creation. The Power of Water held as ice begins to contribute to the creative process by carrying essential matter and assisting cohesion. It also carries away the remnants of the Old Order.

Matter undergoes its penultimate transformation in the autumn as the earth yields it fruits and the cycle of Creation draws towards its close. The cleansing power of Water washes clean the canvas of creation carrying back to The Source those things that have completed their time.

Winter comes. The power of fire is diminished and the earth sleeps as it cools due to the tilt of its axis. Yet as the northern hemisphere leans away from the sun and slips into the silent slumber of winter, the cycle begins anew in the southern hemisphere where the elemental quarters are geographically inverted.

THE SEASONAL GATES

The Seasonal Gates are set between the elemental quarters to represent the flow of the creative energy of the Universe.

The Vernal Gate is set between Fire and Air, representing the rising power of Fire as it is fed by Air. It is seen in the rising of the Sun and the warming of the day and the beginnings of new activity and life as the season changes. Each dawn is a new start, each Spring brings renewal and rebirth in the wake of the transmutational power of fire. Earth yields to the plough, as the chalice accepts the blade and the Goddess joins with the God.

The Summer Gate lies between Air and Earth. As the Fire of Divine Will gathers power it heats the Winds of Reason, stirring its creative currents causing matter to shift into the patterns of life and form, driving the Dust of Ages forward into full fruition as it approaches and melds through the vapours of Water heated and stirred by Fire and Air.

The Autumnal Gate is found between Earth and Water for it is here that we find the culmination and perfection of the process of Creation. It is here that the passion of will and drive of reason are modified by the intuition of Water. It is within and through this mediation that matter can flow flexibly, filling the moulds, fashioned by the intellect and driven by the Fire of Divine Will. Here it is that the Goddess gives birth to form, from the seeds gifted to her by her Consort.

And as the Cycle of Creation turns and flows towards to East the modifying energy of Water slows the transmutational power of Fire, reducing its influence and gradually dissolves the bonds of matter, and the Crone and Devourer return all to the Dust of Ages. Thus the Winter Gate is set between Water and Fire. This is the time of repose. All that is becomes all that was, returning to refuel the Divine Flame as all prepares for the cycle of creation to begin anew.

10 CASTING THE CIRCLE

Only when the space is cleansed and properly prepared can the circle or circles be cast. A single circle is cast for a simple gathering or moot. Double circles are cast for Esbats and simple works such as healings, etc. Triple circles are cast for all major work:
Sabbats
Handfastings
Bonding Ceremonies
Initiations
Sendings Through (Funeral Rites)
And
Invoking the Spirit (The Horned) [God][1]

Each circle cast is aspersed and fumigated with salt water and an appropriate ritual incense mixed and consecrated for the purpose.

CONCERNING THE ASPERGILLUM

Much of the time it is sufficient to asperse the working area by hand, but for the more complex works an aspergillum is advised. An aspergillum most generally appropriate has a handle of hazel or mistletoe to which sprigs of lavender, rosemary and hyssop are bound using threads or ribbons of the Five Elements. For rituals of Sending Through the fifth element thread or ribbon is purple.

Where no aspergil is available add a few drops of oil of lavender, rosemary and hyssop to the water in the aspersorium.

CONCERNING THE ASPERSION AND ASPERSORIUM

The Aspersorium shall be a suitable bowl of white or yellow metal that is reserved solely for the purpose of containing the waters to cleanse the sacred space.

Preparation of the Aspersorium

Having obtained a suitable bowl let it be taken to a fast flowing stream in a hidden place and there let it be fumigated by incenses of Fire and Air.

OPUS

Add the fire incense to the thurible and hold the bowl over the smoke first inverted so that the vapours permeate the interior. Then turn it upright to release the smoke and allow the vessel to be enveloped completely in the elemental fumes.

Speak thus:

By Eternal Fire are you purged of all impurity.
By Eternal Fire is all illusion and deceit destroyed from this vessel.
By Eternal Fire is this vessel prepared for its sacred work.

Clear then the Fire incense from the coals and [add][2] the incense of Air proceeding as before.

Speak Thus:

By the Breath of the Heavens is your true nature now made known:
By the clarity of Elemental Air is your purpose now
revealed; from that which shall be contained within this

sacred vessel shall all virtue and goodness proceed driving away all that is harmful and ill-dignified.

Take then the bowl and plunge it into the stream.

Speak thus:

By the Blood of Creation is your past expunged.
By this same blood are you given new life.

Lift the aspersorium from the waters and say:

From your old existence are you freed. Born again are you to a life of sacred works.

Take then a small stone from the stream's bed and place in the bowl saying:

By sacred earth are you raised renewed by the power of the God and by the grace of our Great Lady Mother Earth.

So mote it be!

Where it is not possible to carry out this work by a stream the aspersorium can be consecrated by immersion in the sea or in consecrated water.

The bowl should be kept wrapped in a cloth of natural white linen, cotton or silk, which has the symbols of the elements embroidered in the elemental colour in each corner with a suitable ambigram for Spirit in the centre.

The Aspersorium Cloth

After each use the aspersorium is cleansed using appropriate cleansing incense and by immersion in blessed or moon-charged water. It is placed in the centre of the cloth [illustrated above] and wrapped in the order and with the words as follows:

By eternal Fire be purged
By Creation's Blood are you made new
By the Breath of Heaven is your
purity of purpose restored
By Mother's grace and favour
shall you be reborn.

Place then both hands upon the cloth and say

In the Spirit of the Great One
are you enfolded that no harm
shall be done thee and no Illusion
or deceit may enter thee.

So mote it be!

Note:

If no stream can be found then the aspersorium can be prepared by immersing it in moon-charged water for the last three days of the waxing moon. When this is completed the stream bed stone can be replaced with a sprinkling of The Dust of Ages.[3]

CONCERNING THE ASPERSIVE

The aspersive is of two types: solar and lunar. Both kinds are prepared using pure stream, distilled or filtered water.

OPUS SOLARIS

Using water drawn as described and consecrated in the manner of The Art, fill a glass or earthen vessel and [add][4] in a few grains of consecrated salt. Place in the water:

              7 Rowan berries
              3 sprigs Rosemary
              1 piece Ginseng Root

Place the flask in the light of the rising sun with words:~

> Lord of Light, Bringer of Life
> Vouchsafe and bless this, thy creature of the kind of Water.
> Imbue it with Thy strength, light and power.
> That it shall become suited to cleanse and protect whatsoever
> It shall touch.
> So Mote it Be!

Repeat the process for three days. Each time remove or cover the vessel at or just after midday so that the aspersive is exposed only to the strengthening light.

When the process of consecration and charging is completed, strain the aspersive through a suitably blessed linen or cotton cloth. Preserve and dry the solids and reduced them to ash by smouldering on charcoal. The resultant residue can then be added to the Dust of Ages.[3]

Note:

If an earthen vessel is used for this work it must be a bowl so that the light of the Sun may fall directly on to the aspersive. If the flask for storing the aspersive is of glass it should be kept covered by a cloth of white linen or cotton that has been consecrated and marked as previously shown.

OPUS PER LUNAN

As with the Solar aspersive, the Lunar aspersive is prepared using water from the same source and the basics of preparation are the same. A flask of glass or earthen bowl is used for the consecration process. Add salt as before, and then add:

> 7 pieces of Calamus Root
> 3 Eucalyptus leaves
> 5 Willow leaves

Place the vessel in the light of the waxing moon taking care to begin the work two nights before the moon reaches full. Speak Thus:

> Hail Lady of the Night
> Light of our Dark Times.
> Vouchsafe and bless this
> Thy daughter in the kind of Water

Imbue her with thy grace, purity and clarity
That she shall become suited to cleanse and protect and purify
Whatsoever she shall touch.
So Mote it Be!

Repeat this three times up to full moon. Each morning before dawn or at the end of each blessing the liquid must be covered so that it is not exposed to sunlight.

When the work is completed the aspersive must be strained through a cloth as with the Solar aspersive. The solids shall be preserved and dried as before and then smouldered to ash after which they are mixed with the Dust of Ages.[3]

Note:

As with the Solar Aspersive, if the Lunar Aspersive is to be stored in a glass vessel it must be kept covered with a consecrated cloth of linen, cotton, or silk.

The aspersives can be re-charged periodically either by adding freshly blessed aspersive if the current supply is running low or by exposing it to its power source and repeating the prayer of consecration.

11 THE CASTING AND INVOKATIONS

There are several ways to cast circles. It can be done using a wand, stave, sword or athame. Generally speaking witches will use blades. Wizards and Sorcerers and the like use wands and staves, using the athame to sever the veil or to open a gateway in the circle or circles.

Single Circles

The most common ceremonial circle is a single cast and this is suitable for most work as it is used solely to provide a clear consecrated space in which the magus will carry out his task.

Double Circles

These are cast when working with the God or Goddess. The first circle is cast to provide a sacred area and the second to create the temple for the God and/or Goddess is cast within the sacred space.

Triple Circles

These are cast when working with the powers, the deities and with the ancestors.

INCANTING THE CIRCLES

A single line in circle round
Scribed neath the sky upon this ground
Shall stand and serve as a sacred wall
And safe within stand one and all.

The second circle cast about
Drives all trace of evil out
Goddess below us, God above
Enfold us in your strength and love

Thrice cast shall form the final wall
Ancestors and friends come heed the call
Come forth in love and perfect trust
To witness this work and stand with us.

So Mote It Be!

Asperge again with salt and water and fumigate with the ritual incense.

CONSOLIDATING THE CIRCLES

Three circles cast now join as one
On sacred earth 'neath moon and sun,
Shall not be sundered or undone
Until this blessed Work is run

So Mote it Be!

Once [the circle is][1] cast, and where necessary consolidated, the Quarters are then called. This is done to invoke the Spirits of the Quarters. Unless the Guardians of the Quarters are either familiar with the magician(s) or have been approached through the appropriate method of propitiation, they should not be invoked directly. Similarly, unless there is an established relationship between the magus and the Towers and Lords of the Watchtower [these][2] should not be invoked.

Never invoke the Quarters or the Watchers with the words "Ye Lords and Ladies of the Watchtower…" The intelligences of the Towers, though they may be perceived as possessing feminine qualities or aspects, are exclusively masculine.

Remember: If you look into The Abyss, It may look back.[3]

In invoking the Quarters it is wise to use a generic salutation such as "brothers" or "spirits". This approach is taken so that the call becomes an open invitation to the Guardians and denizens of the Towers alike and provides the practitioner with the opportunity to build a relationship with the higher, stronger Powers.

This basic Invokation is composed in couplets so that the energy will flow with the rhythm of the chant. It is also designed so that those others who are working at the quarter can also pick up the rhythm of the Invokation.

This final part of the Invokation is spoken by the magus in cases where the ceremony is the work of a group.

THE INVOKATION OF THE QUARTERS

Brothers of fire and passion burn bright.
Let you love and grace strengthen this sacred Rite.

Spirits of heaven's winds breath swift and sure,
Draw close with your love that no evil endure.

Spirits of Water come swift to my side
And now [….][3] this space in the wake of your tide.

Brothers that furnish the earth 'neath our feet
Draw close and vouchsafe the place that we meet

[For a more detailed Invokation of the Quarters, refer to pages 48 and 49]

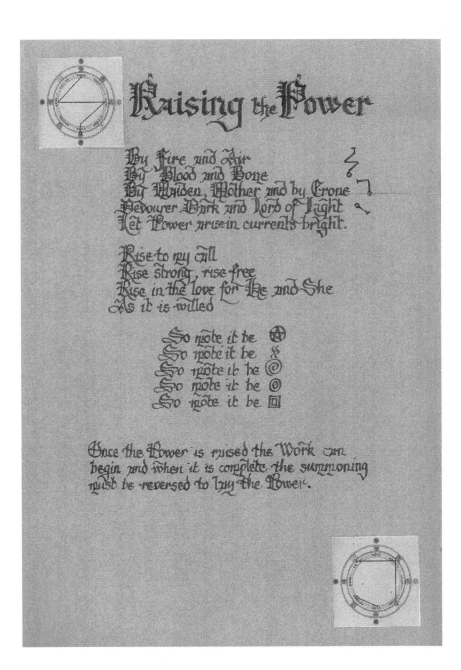

Raising the Power

By Fire and Air
By Blood and Bone
By Maiden, Mother and by Crone
Devourer Dark and Lord of Light
Let Power arise in currents bright.

Rise to my call
Rise strong, rise free
Rise in the love for He and She
As it is willed

So mote it be
So mote it be
So mote it be
So mote it be
So mote it be

Once the Power is raised the Work can
begin and when it is complete the summoning
must be reversed to lay the Power.

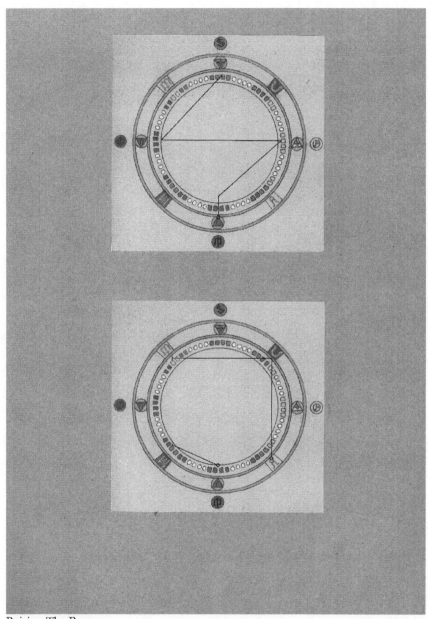

Raising The Power

INVOKING THE GOD

By the flame that burneth bright
O Horned One!
We call thy name into the night
O Horned One!

Thee we invoke by the moon led sea
By the standing stone and the twisted tree
Thee we invoke where gather thine own
By the nameless shrine forgotten and lone

Come where the round of the dance is trod
Horn and hoof of the goat-foot God
By moonlit meadow on dusky hill
When the haunted wood is hushed and still

Come to the charm of the chanted prayer
As the moon bewitches the midnight air
Evoke thy powers, that potent bide
In shining stream and secret tide

In fiery flame by starlight pale
In shadowy host that ride the gale
And by the fern-brakes fairy-haunted
Of forests wild and wood enchanted

Come! O Come!
To the heartbeats drum!
Come to us who gather below
When the broad white moon is climbing slow

Through the stars to the heavens height
We hear thy hoofs on the wind of night
As black tree branches shake and sigh
By joy and terror we know thee nigh

We speak the spell thy power unlocks
At Solstice, Sabbat, and Equinox!

Doreen Valiente
"Witchcraft for Tomorrow"
Reproduced with kind permission of the publishers, Robert Hale Ltd.

LICENSE TO DEPART

Brothers of Earth who formed this space,
Keep safe our path as we leave this place.
Return with our love to where you dwell.
We bid you now Hail and Farewell.

Spirits of Water who cleanse our hearts
In peace you came, in peace depart.
Return with our love to where you dwell.
We bid you now Hail and Farewell.

Spirits of Air, inspiration and grace,
With peace you fill our sacred space
Return with our love to where you dwell.
We bid you now Hail and Farewell.

Brothers of fire, warmth and light
Whose strength informs this sacred Rite
Return with our love to where you dwell.
We bid you now Hail and Farewell.

Nikki Dorakis

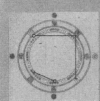

Laying the Power

Lord of Light, Devourer Dark
I now return the Sacred Spark
To Crone and Mother and sacred Maid
Power returns with love engraved.
By bone and blood, by air and fire
Power called must now retire.

Return within the sacred Earth.
Return to She who gave you birth.
Return to He who gave you force
Sleep now for you have run your course.
Return to The Source and there remain
Until I call you forth again.

Rest in the love of He and She
As it is willed

So mote it be
So mote it be
So mote it be
So mote it be
So mote it be

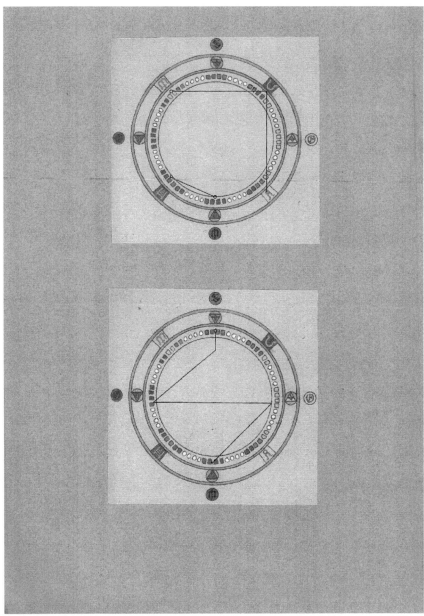

Laying the Power

DISSOLUTION

What once joined I now unweave
What was one shall now be three
Preparing now to be undone
For now the working time is run

GATHERING IN

Circle wide and circle round
Cast upon this sacred ground
I call you back I call you in
From without and from within

Third cast of three I now unweave
Ancestors and friends now take your leave
Go with our love to where you dwell
In Peace Depart
Hail and Farewell

The second cast I now unweave
Lord of Light and Darksome Queen
Returning to your realms unseen
Go with our love to where you dwell
In Peace Depart
Hail and Farewell

First cast of three I now unweave
As do I now take my leave
Our love endures within this place
But of nought else shall be a trace
Nought now remains to feel or see
As is my will
So Mote it be.

EDITOR'S NOTES

Part One   **Rites of Passage**

Chapter 1   Why We Need the Rite of Passage

Note [1]   This word was omitted from the original text.

Note[2]   See Foreword, Page 7 for further information on this issue

Chapter 2   The Planetary Influences

Note [1]   Age 13 – the age of the Bar Mitzvah in the Jewish Tradition, at which point the Boy is recognised as having the same rights as an adult Man. He is now seen as morally, and ethically, culpable for his own decisions and actions.

Chapter 3   The Movement to Manhood

Note[1]   This word was omitted from the original text.

Chapter 4   Initiation: The Precepts

Note[1]   This word was omitted from the original text.

Note[2]   The scored out words were removed in this text for grammatical reasons, and have been included only to indicate where a change has been made to the original text.

Note[3]   This word was omitted from the original text.

Note[4]   This word was omitted from the original text.

Note[5]   The scored out words were removed in this text for grammatical reasons, and have been included only to indicate where a change has been made to the original text.

Chapter 5   Ethics

Note [1]   This word was omitted from the original text

Note[2]   This appears to be an adaptation around the themes
                 contained in Doreen Valiente's Wiccan Rede. This was first
                 recorded as a '8 word couplet' in 1964 *"Eight words the Wiccan
                 Rede fulfil, An it harm none, do what ye will"* and Aleister
                 Crowley's Book of the Law *"Do what thou wilt shall be the whole
                 of the Law….Love is the law, love under will"* (Liber Al vel Legis,
                 1904).The phrase in various forms is in current common use
                 within modern neo-pagan communities.

Note[3]   Obviously a reference to the Wiccan Rede (see above Note[2])

Note[4]   This word was unintelligible in original text.

Part Two   **Ritual**

Chapter 6   Ritual

Note [1]   Added for clarity

Note [2]   Added for clarity

Chapter 7

Note[1,2,3,4]   These words were encoded, and were not legible in the
                 original text.

Note[5]   A common form of challenge when entering the circle,
                 which also appeared in a similar form in *The Craft*: a 1996
                 film directed by Andrew Fleming, and written by Andrew
                 Fleming and Peter Filardi.

Note[6]   A traditional oath, often used in modern wedding
                 ceremonies. Author unknown.

Note[7]   Omitted from original text. Added here for clarity.

Note[8,9]   Omitted from original text. Added here for clarity.

Chapter 8   Cleansing the Space

Note[1]   North

Note[2]   South

Note[3]   East

Note[4]   West

Note[5]   Added to the text to clarify that the final act should be
                   repeated at this stage.

Note[6,7]   The original written script stated East. However the symbol
                   used is that of West/Water and the text has been   altered to
                   reflect this.

Note[8]   North

Chapter 10   Casting the Circle

Note[1]   Omitted in the original text but added here to clarify
                   meaning.
Note[2]   Omitted in the original text but added here to clarify
                   meaning.
Note[3]   About the Dust of Ages
                   There are several references earlier in the book to the Dust
                   of Ages as a reference to the cosmos or universal energy
                   from which we all come and to which we shall all return.

                   In this context however, the term "Dust of Ages" refers to
                   the collection of the burnt remains of plant matter and
                   incenses used in the course of magical works. The remains
                   are collected in a securable receptacle, preferably made of
                   wood, and kept. This can then be used to represent the Dust
                   of Ages or the Element of Earth, in rituals such as that
                   described in the notes on the preparation of the Aspergillum.

Note[4]	Omitted in the original text but added here to clarify meaning.

Chapter 11   The Casting & Invokations

Note[1]	Omitted in the original text but added here to clarify meaning.
Note[2]	Omitted in the original text but added here to clarify meaning.
Note[3]	Possibly an adaption of text used in Nietzsche's (1886) *Beyond Good and Evil* "And if you gaze for long into an abyss, the abyss gazes also into you."
Note[4]	Unintelligible in original text

ABOUT THE AUTHOR

Nikki Dorakis was born in 1954 on the Isle of Wight, England. He left the Isle of Wight at age 18 and travelled the world extensively, meeting and discussing with many priests, shamans, witches, sages and holy men from a variety of paths. As a Pagan Priest and an ordained Minister of the Church of Spiritual Humanism, Nikki became concerned with the lack of spiritual guidance for men and, in particular, the effect of modern societal changes on the male psyche, and their self-perceived role within modern Western culture. To this end he decided to write a book on male rites of passage and the development of positive and sustainable qualities and attributes among the Brotherhood Of Men.

Drawing upon his years of experience as an occultist and ceremonial magician, his own faith and the teachings of various priests, shamans, druids, witches, and spiritual seekers he met during the course of his life, Nikki produced a handwritten and illuminated manuscript on the subject of the Male Mysteries, which is now reproduced here in paperback for a wider audience.

Nikki passed into spirit in 2013, having published a fantasy fiction collection and leaving a vast collection of occult and esoteric journals, artwork, and books.

His work can be obtained via the publisher, The Wizard's Wheel on their website at www.wizardswheel.co.uk and via Amazon.

8798787R10049

Printed in Great Britain
by Amazon.co.uk, Ltd.,
Marston Gate.